GERMAN SUPERCARS

PORSCHE • AUDI • MERCEDES

Paul Mason

PowerKiDS
press

Published in 2019 by The Rosen
Publishing Group, Inc.
29 East 21st Street, New York, NY 10010

Cataloging-in-Publication Data

Names: Mason, Paul.
Title: German supercars: Porsche, Audi,
Mercedes / Paul Mason.
Description: New York : PowerKids Press,
2019. | Series: Supercars | Includes
glossary and index.
Identifiers: LCCN ISBN 9781538338872
(pbk.) | ISBN 9781538338865 (library bound)
| ISBN 9781538338889 (6 pack)
Subjects: LCSH: Sports cars--Juvenile
literature. | Automobiles, Racing--Juvenile
literature.
Classification: LCC TL236.M29 2019 | DDC
629.222--dc23

Manufactured in the United States of
America

CPSIA Compliance Information: Batch
CS18PK: For Further Information contact
Rosen Publishing, New York, New York at
1-800-237-9932.

Executive editor: Adrian Cole
Series designer: Mayer Media
Design manager: Peter Scoulding
Picture researcher: Diana Morris

Picture Credits:

Abstract/Shutterstock: 10b. AnabelA88/
Shutterstock: 7b, 9t, 19tr, 21bl, 25b.
Apollo Arrow: 6-7, 7t. Artzz/Dreamstime:
3b, 30br. Audi: 1t, 3c,8c, 8-9, 10-11, 11b.
Pieter B/autogesport: 29cl. Bayerische
Motoren Werke AG: 1b, 5t, 12-13, 13t,
14-15, 15t. Ermess/Shutterstock: 30cl.
Matthew Gaussage/Alamy: 4-5. LOTEC :
28t. Mercedes-Benz: 16-17, 17t, 18t, 18-19,
28c, 29b, 31. Sam Moores/Shutterstock:
front cover t. Porsche A.G: 3t, 20-21. 21br,
22-23, 23t, 24-25, 24b, 26t, 26-27, 29t,
32. Alexandre Prévot Photographie: 28b.
Darin Schnarbel © 2012. Courtesy of RM
Auctions: 29cr. Superstock: 4t. Jordan Tan/
Dreamstime: 30tl. Denis Van der Water/
Dreamstime: 30tr. Miro Vrlilk Photography/
Shutterstock: front cover b. Wikimedia
Commons: 30b.

Contents

Contents

Words highlighted in **bold** can be found in the glossary

GERMANY:
BIRTHPLACE OF THE CAR

In 1885, a German engineer named Karl Benz made a vehicle called a *Motorwagen*. It had three wheels, seats like a horse-drawn carriage, and a gas engine. It was the first gas-powered car.

It may not look much like a supercar, but this 1885 Benz Motorwagen *was the start of the story of the car.*

SUPERCAR MANUFACTURERS

Karl Benz's company would one day become Mercedes Benz, which now makes some of the world's greatest supercars. They are not the only supercar makers in Germany, though. Audi and BMW also build cutting-edge supercars, as do specialist firms such as Apollo and 9ff. But the most famous German supercar maker is Porsche. Porsche has been making high-performance cars ever since it released the first 911 model, in 1964.

Engine: most supercars have **mid-mounted** engines, but the 911's engine is rear mounted

Price Tag...

The first 911s cost the equivalent of about $6,000. Today, a 1964 Porsche 911 would cost you nearly $200,000 — possibly a lot more, depending on what condition the car is in. That's almost double the price of a brand-new 911 Carrera!

Engine layout: the 911 has a **flat-6** engine, which is unusual because most supercars have a V-shaped engine layout

Seating: the 911 is a **2+2**: it has two front seats, and two small seats in the back. This makes the 911 one of only a few supercars with room for more than one passenger!

Drive: like many supercars, the 911 has rear-wheel **drive**

TOP SPEED
125 mph
(200 km/h)

0–60 MPH
9.1 seconds

MAX POWER
96 kw
(129 bhp) @ 6,100 rpm

MAX **TORQUE**
174 Nm
(128lb/ft) @ 4,600 rpm

Max RPM:
6,100

Engine:
1991 cc flat-6

Weight:
2,380 lbs

Fuel use per 60 miles (estimated):
21 liters

CO2:
not known

Gearbox:
5-speed

Drive:
rear wheels

Main body:
steel

Frame:
steel

Braking:
hydraulic discs

The BMW 503 (1954) **convertible** *was made in limited numbers, largely because production costs were too high.*

JUST WHAT *IS* A SUPERCAR?

There is no agreed definition of what makes a car a supercar. It could be some or all of these things:

- really expensive
- made in tiny numbers
- as high-performance as possible
- very fast, and probably very light
- tricky to drive
- not ideal for daily driving

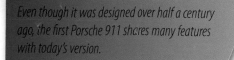

Even though it was designed over half a century ago, the first Porsche 911 shares many features with today's version.

Body shape: although it looks different from a modern 911, if you park the two side-by-side you can see they are related

APOLLO
ARROW

The name alone is enough to make you want to see an Arrow. And if you ever see one howl past at 220 mph, you will understand where they got the name. This car flies! The Arrow was designed by Roland Gumpert as a race-ready, but **street-legal**, car.

The Arrow's styling is inspired by sharks. Not only a shark's streamlined shape and speed through the water — but also its aggressive, attacking nature. When the car starts, its engine snaps and snarls as the driver pushes the accelerator. The sound of the burbling exhausts is loud even when the Arrow isn't moving. The roar as the Arrow pulls away is deafening! You won't hear it for long, though — the Arrow can hit over 120 mph in 8.8 seconds.

The Arrow was developed from one of the world's fastest cars, the Gumpert Apollo. In 2009 the Gumpert set a new record for speed around Germany's famous **Nürburgring** track. Many European supercar makers test their cars at "The Ring," and being fastest around it is a big deal. The Arrow is more powerful than the Gumpert, so it may grab the record back.

Arrow-like **aerodynamics** reduce drag and improve **downforce**

Price Tag...

Only 100 Arrows are being produced, and are expected to have a list price of around $1.3 million. You'll get a custom car for your money, though, plus some special features.

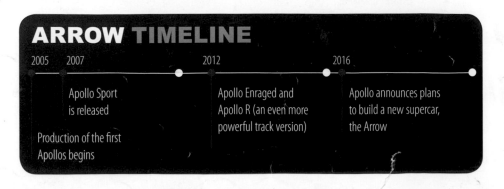

ARROW TIMELINE

2005	2007	2012	2016
	Apollo Sport is released	Apollo Enraged and Apollo R (an even more powerful track version)	Apollo announces plans to build a new supercar, the Arrow
	Production of the first Apollos begins		

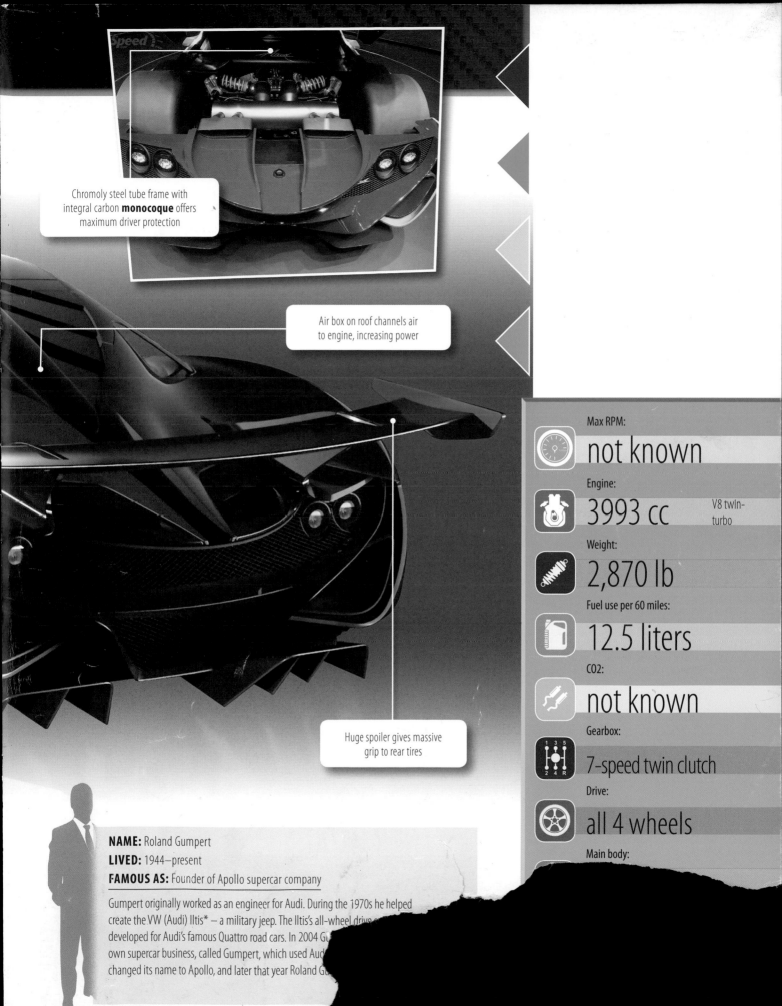

Chromoly steel tube frame with integral carbon **monocoque** offers maximum driver protection

Air box on roof channels air to engine, increasing power

Huge spoiler gives massive grip to rear tires

Max RPM:
not known

Engine:
3993 cc
V8 twin-turbo

Weight:
2,870 lb

Fuel use per 60 miles:
12.5 liters

CO2:
not known

Gearbox:
7-speed twin clutch

Drive:
all 4 wheels

Main body:

NAME: Roland Gumpert
LIVED: 1944–present
FAMOUS AS: Founder of Apollo supercar company

Gumpert originally worked as an engineer for Audi. During the 1970s he helped create the VW (Audi) Iltis* – a military jeep. The Iltis's all-wheel drive developed for Audi's famous Quattro road cars. In 2004 G own supercar business, called Gumpert, which used Aud changed its name to Apollo, and later that year Roland G

*Iltis is German for "polecat," an animal similar to the weasel.

AUDI
R8 V10 QUATTRO PLUS

When the R8 was released in 2006, its high performance was a surprise to some, including other supercar manufacturers. Audi's first supercar was immediately voted the best in the world.

Factory: Neckarsulm, Baden-Württemberg, Germany

In 2015 the original R8 was replaced by an almost completely new version. It has a bigger engine and is more powerful. Audi owns the Italian supercar manufacturer Lamborghini. Some of the technology for the R8 comes from the Lamborghini Huracán — including the turbo-charged V10 engine.

Despite using the same engine, the Quattro Plus is very different from a Huracán. It is easy to drive, for starters. The Quattro Plus has room for a tiny bit of luggage. It can also be driven over speed bumps without getting stuck!

In 2016, an open-topped R8 Spyder was released. At the touch of a button, the Spyder's roof folds itself up and disappears. The Spyder is slightly heavier and slower than the **coupe**, but a lot more glamorous.

The V10 engine shared by the R8 and Lamborghini Huracán.

The 5.2-liter engine delivers 601 bhp through all four wheels

Fixed carbon-fiber rear wing only appears on the V10 Quattro Plus

IN·R 8100

R8 TIMELINE

2006 — First Audi R8, with a V8 engine and other borrowed technology from the Lamborghini Gallardo, is released

2015 — Open-topped R8 Spyder is released

2016 — Almost completely new R8, now based on the Lamborghini Huracán, comes out

---

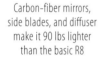

NAME: August Horch
LIVED: 1868–1951
FAMOUS AS: Founder of Audi

Horch worked for Karl Benz, the founder of Mercedes Benz, before he began his own car company. *Horch* means "listen" in German. Audi got its name because Horch's old business partners took him to court to stop him using his own name for the company. So instead, he used the Latin for "listen" – *audi*.

What's it like to drive?

Like a dream. Like a far out, freaky, fast-forward-engaged, too many e-numbers dream [of] howling madness and gorgeous g-forces. In other words, it's pretty fast.

– carmagazine.co.uk review

Carbon-fiber mirrors, side blades, and diffuser make it 90 lbs lighter than the basic R8

Laser headlights reach twice as far as normal **LED** lights

Price Tag...

It will cost you around $158,000 for the basic R8, more for the open-topped Spyder version. The R8 V10 Plus, which is the fastest R8, costs from around $177,000.

Max RPM:
8,500

Engine:
5204 cc V10

Weight:
3,600 lbs

Fuel use per 60 miles:
12.3 liters

CO2:
287 g/km

Gearbox:
7-speed dual-clutch automatic

Drive:
all 4 wheels

Main body:
aluminum

Frame:
aluminum-carbon monocoque

Braking:
carbon-ceramic

AUDI
TT RS

Audi's RS cars are high-performance versions of its normal cars. The TT RS is fitted with a souped-up **inline 5** engine – plus a whole lot of other speedy features.

The inline 5 engine is famous among Audi lovers. An engine like this was first used in the Audi Quattro in 1980. The Quattro, as it was known, was the car to beat in **WRC**. It was famous for the unique noise of its engine. When the first TT RS appeared in 2009, Audi fans rejoiced to see that the inline 5 was back.

In 2016, a new TT RS was released. It was lighter and more powerful than the original. The power of the lightweight aluminum engine was controlled by a highly developed computer system. This made the TT RS scarily fast, but also drivable.

Large fixed rear spoiler

Suspension can be changed by the RS's computers in milliseconds, adapting to how and where the car is being driven

Double-pipe exhaust system maximizes the noise of the famous 5-cylinder engine

NAME: Michèle Mouton
LIVED: 1951–present
FAMOUS AS: Groundbreaking rally driver

Michèle Mouton is one of only a few female drivers who have made it to the top in rallying. She started as a co-driver, but soon became a driver. In 1981, driving an Audi Quattro, she won the Rally San Remo and became the first woman to win a WRC rally. In 1982, Mouton won three more rallies for Audi, and finished second to Walter Röhrl (see page 25) in the World Championship.

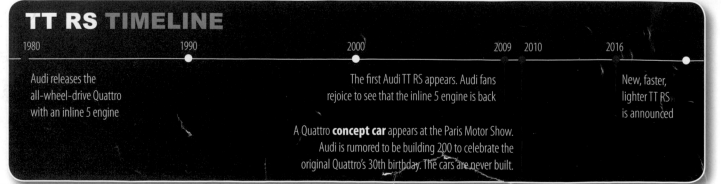

TT RS TIMELINE

1980	1990	2000	2009	2010	2016

1980 — Audi releases the all-wheel-drive Quattro with an inline 5 engine

2000 — A Quattro **concept car** appears at the Paris Motor Show. Audi is rumored to be building 200 to celebrate the original Quattro's 30th birthday. The cars are never built.

2009 — The first Audi TT RS appears. Audi fans rejoice to see that the inline 5 engine is back

2016 — New, faster, lighter TT RS is announced

If a sports exhaust is fitted, the driver can push a dashboard button to control the noise

Price Tag...

The coupe version starts at around $80,000. So, it's about 45 percent of the price of an R8 (see pages 8–9) and is only half a second slower to reach 60 mph. That's a good value!

Large front air intakes help cool the powerful engine

What's it like to drive?

That first surge of acceleration will leave you in no doubt as to how stunningly fast the little coupe is. The power feels totally contained, however, with the Quattro deploying every ounce of the 394 bhp. It's bursting with energy...

– www.evo.co.uk review

THE TT RS ROADSTER

Audi also makes a convertible version of the TT RS, known as the Roadster. This car takes 0.2 seconds longer to reach 60 mph. The convertible roof is electronically controlled and it can be lowered or raised while the car is moving. You can't control the roof while driving at top speed, though. To do that, you have to be driving 31 mph or slower.

Max RPM:
7,000

Engine:
2500 cc   turbo-charged inline 5

Weight:
3,175 lbs

Fuel use per 60 miles:
9 liters

CO2:
200 g/km

Gearbox:
7-speed dual-clutch automatic

Drive:
all 4 wheels

Main body:
aluminum and steel (est.)

Frame:
aluminum

Braking:
aluminum (optional carbon-ceramic front brakes)

BMW

i8

Factory: Leipzig, Saxony, Germay

Fans of **Formula E** will recognize this BMW right away — the i8 is used as a **safety car** during races. Whenever there is a problem on the track, the i8 zooms out and the race cars form a line behind it.

The i8 is an unusual supercar, because it is a gas-electric **hybrid**. A few other supercars (the McLaren P1 and the Ferrari LaFerrari) are also hybrids, but those rely mainly on a huge, powerful gas engine, only using their electric motors for an extra boost of power when needed. The i8 is different. It has a tiny, 1.5-liter engine — the same as is used in a Mini. The rest of its power comes from electric motors.

The i8 is less powerful than other supercars, and carries a heavy electric battery. This means the rest of the car has to be super light. Many parts are made of lightweight carbon fiber, to reduce weight as much as possible.

Classic gull-wing supercar design

In Sport mode, the noise of the gas engine is sent to speakers in the cabin, as a way of making the car sound more exciting

What's it like to drive?

Flooring the throttle gives you a smooth and muscular surge of acceleration, accompanied by a sci-fi whine from the electric motor and a deep, throaty growl from the three-cylinder engine.

– Review from *autoexpress.co.uk*

Price Tag...

It will cost you around $152,000 to buy a new i8. This is not one of the supercars that are worth more after you have bought it, though: used i8s start at about $99,000.

i8 TIMELINE

2009 2014 2017

A diesel-powered concept car of the i8 appears at the 2009 Frankfurt Motor Show

Gas-electric hybrid i8s go on sale

Updated, faster i8S

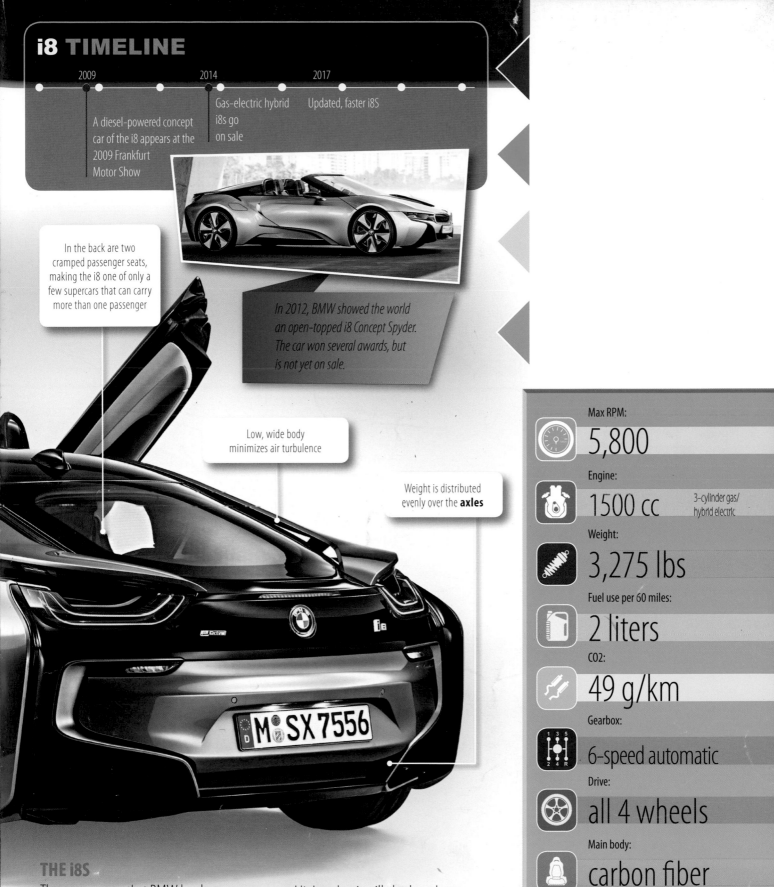

In the back are two cramped passenger seats, making the i8 one of only a few supercars that can carry more than one passenger

In 2012, BMW showed the world an open-topped i8 Concept Spyder. The car won several awards, but is not yet on sale.

Low, wide body minimizes air turbulence

Weight is distributed evenly over the **axles**

THE i8S

There are rumors that BMW has been developing a lighter, more powerful version of the i8, called the i8S. Only 100 are planned. The i8S was first designed to celebrate BMW's 100th birthday, in 2016. It is not only said to be more powerful and lighter, but it will also have better suspension, brakes and aerodynamics. Overall, these changes would mean the car could reach 60 mph in under 4 seconds.

Max RPM:
5,800

Engine:
1500 cc 3-cylinder gas/ hybrid electric

Weight:
3,275 lbs

Fuel use per 60 miles:
2 liters

CO2:
49 g/km

Gearbox:
6-speed automatic

Drive:
all 4 wheels

Main body:
carbon fiber

Frame:
carbon fiber

Braking:
carbon-ceramic

BMW
M6 COUPE COMPETITION

The M6 Coupe Competition is built for speed and luxury. The suspension has a "comfort" setting, there is space for three passengers, and it even has a trunk that will carry luggage! All that ... and it still reaches 60 mph 2.4 seconds faster than a Porsche Panamera.

Factory: Dingolfing, Bavaria, Germany

The Coupe Competition is based on a standard M6, with more power. The M6 is a "grand tourer," designed to drive — very quickly, but comfortably — over long distances. The Competition has a V8 engine, and is fitted with suspension and other features to help the driver handle the extra speed.

Price Tag...

Handing over about $145,000 will mean you can drive away in a new M6 Competition.

Drivers can choose to change gear themselves using "paddles" behind the steering wheel, or let the car's computer decide when to change

Large air intakes channel air to the engine and brakes for cooling, and aid aerodynamics

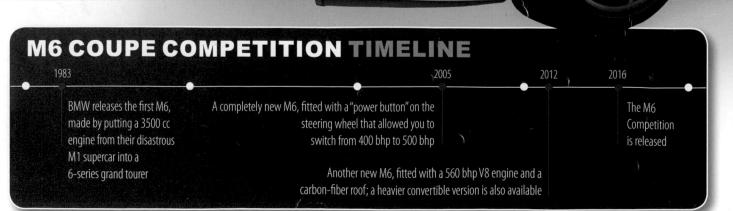

M6 COUPE COMPETITION TIMELINE

1983		2005	2012	2016
BMW releases the first M6, made by putting a 3500 cc engine from their disastrous M1 supercar into a 6-series grand tourer	A completely new M6, fitted with a "power button" on the steering wheel that allowed you to switch from 400 bhp to 500 bhp			The M6 Competition is released

Another new M6, fitted with a 560 bhp V8 engine and a carbon-fiber roof; a heavier convertible version is also available

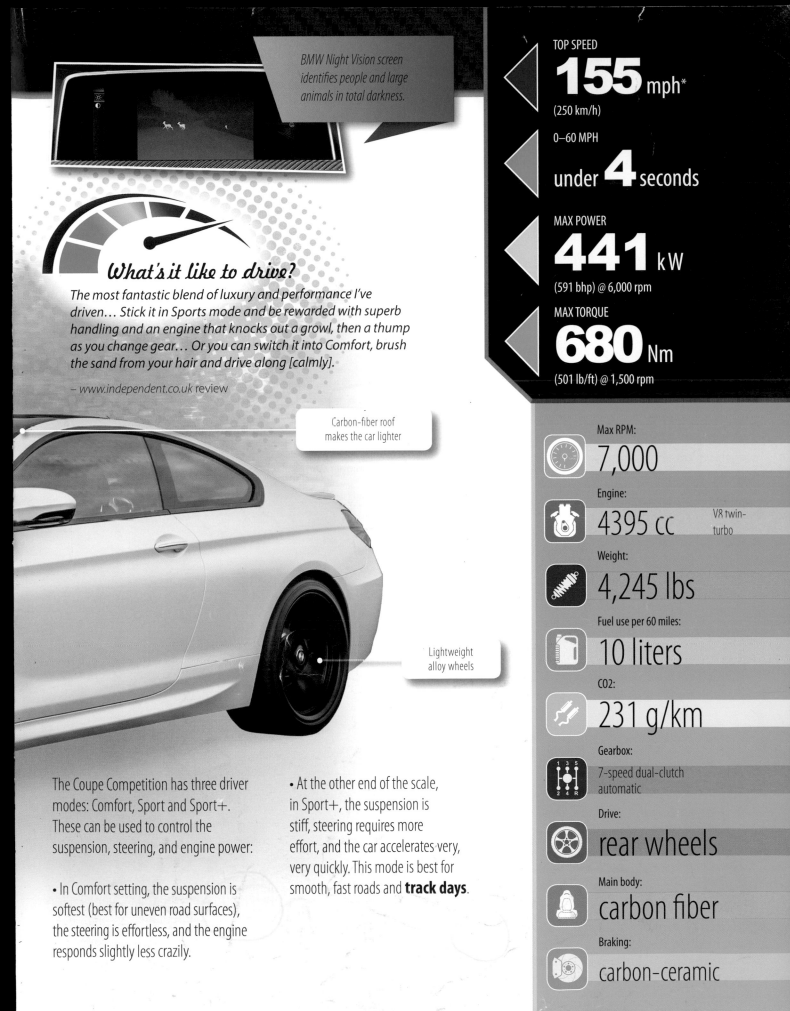

BMW Night Vision screen identifies people and large animals in total darkness.

What's it like to drive?

The most fantastic blend of luxury and performance I've driven… Stick it in Sports mode and be rewarded with superb handling and an engine that knocks out a growl, then a thump as you change gear… Or you can switch it into Comfort, brush the sand from your hair and drive along [calmly].

– www.independent.co.uk review

Carbon-fiber roof makes the car lighter

Lightweight alloy wheels

The Coupe Competition has three driver modes: Comfort, Sport and Sport+. These can be used to control the suspension, steering, and engine power:

• In Comfort setting, the suspension is softest (best for uneven road surfaces), the steering is effortless, and the engine responds slightly less crazily.

• At the other end of the scale, in Sport+, the suspension is stiff, steering requires more effort, and the car accelerates very, very quickly. This mode is best for smooth, fast roads and **track days**.

TOP SPEED
155 mph*
(250 km/h)

0–60 MPH
under **4** seconds

MAX POWER
441 kW
(591 bhp) @ 6,000 rpm

MAX TORQUE
680 Nm
(501 lb/ft) @ 1,500 rpm

Max RPM:
7,000

Engine:
4395 cc   V8 twin-turbo

Weight:
4,245 lbs

Fuel use per 60 miles:
10 liters

CO_2:
231 g/km

Gearbox:
7-speed dual-clutch automatic

Drive:
rear wheels

Main body:
carbon fiber

Braking:
carbon-ceramic

*Can be boosted to 189 mph (304 kph) with M Driver pack

MERCEDES-AMG
GT-S

Whenever you see the letters AMG on a car, you know it will be special. AMG specializes in taking any Mercedes that's already fast and making it even faster.

AMG turns sports cars into supercars by making all kinds of changes. They modify the suspension, aerodynamics, and interior, for example. But AMG is most famous for its engines. Each engine is built by a single worker, and every AMG engine is engraved with the signature of the worker who built it. AMG engines are not only used by Mercedes, they are also fitted in the Pagani Zonda supercar.

Factory: Affalterbach, Baden-Württemberg, Germany

Gear shifts can be fully automatic, or controlled by the driver using steering-wheel paddles

Drive mode can be set to Comfort (which is quietest, softest, best for long distances), Sport, Sport+ or Race (hardest, loudest, and best for the racetrack)

Rear spoiler can be raised to increase downforce

Exhaust noise can be controlled by the driver, who can open or close flaps in the exhaust to change the noise

Front-mid-mounted engine (behind the front axle but in front of the driver) helps share weight almost equally between all four wheels

What's it like to drive?

This is a modern-day muscle car. It's Merc's Mustang. You sense this when you drive it… It feels raw. Much more raw than any other Mercedes and any of the other cars that you can buy for this sort of money. It feels … extremely exciting.

– Jeremy Clarkson review at *www.driving.co.uk*

Engine fitted with an
ECO **stop-start system**

AMG GT-S TIMELINE

1995   2008   2015

AMG begin to release high-performance versions of the latest Mercedes SL 2-seaters

The AMG GT-S is released

SL 73 AMG, the most powerful SL model yet made; this car used the same engine as a Pagani Zonda. Only 85 SL 73s were ever made, and they are now very rare.

An AMG GT-S being used as the safety car at the Malaysia Grand Prix.

The GT-S is a tuned-up version of the AMG-Mercedes GT — a very fast "grand touring" car. The GT-S has more power, and the driver can adjust the engine, suspension, and steering settings to make it perform better on a racetrack. Even so, the GT-S is still comfortable enough to drive on city streets or across the country.

Price Tag...

The AMG GT-S starts at about $165,000. If you have not got quite that much, the less powerful AMG GT starts at about $140,000. But why would you want a less powerful version? Keep saving!

TOP SPEED
193 mph
(310 km/h)

0–60 MPH
3.8 seconds

MAX POWER
375 kW
(503 bhp) @ 6,250 rpm

MAX TORQUE
650 Nm
(479 lb/ft) @ 4,750 rpm

Max RPM:
7,000

Engine:
3982 cc   V8 twin-turbo

Weight:
3,460 lbs

Fuel use per 60 miles:
9.6 liters

CO2:
224 g/km

Gearbox:
7-speed dual-clutch automatic

Drive:
rear wheels

Main body:
aluminum

Frame:
aluminum composite

Braking:
carbon-ceramic

MERCEDES-AMG
SLS

When the SLS came out in 2010, Mercedes fans got very excited. Its design was based on one of the most famous Mercedes ever: the 300 SL Gullwing.

Factory: Affalterbach, Baden-Württemberg, Germany

The Mercedes 300 SL was the design inspiration for the SLS.

Price Tag...

When it appeared, the AMG SLS started at around $225,000. It is no longer possible to buy a new SLS, and used ones cost about the same as the original price. That might seem like a lot, but not compared to the cost of a used 300 SL Gullwing. One of those sold at auction in 2012 for about $4.8 million.

SUPERCAR CONTENDER

The first supercar is usually said to be the Lamborghini Miura – but the Gullwing is another contender. It was a road-going version of the car that won the 1952 Le Mans 24-hour race. Mercedes called it a "race car for the road."

AMG SLS TIMELINE

1953
Mercedes create the 300 SL from their Le Mans-winning race car. Elements of its V12 engine are taken from a World War II fighter plane, the Messerschmitt 109E.

2009
The AMG SLS is released, featuring a similar gullwing design but with a V8 engine

2014
AMG ends production of the SLS with the GT Final Edition – supercar fans everywhere weep

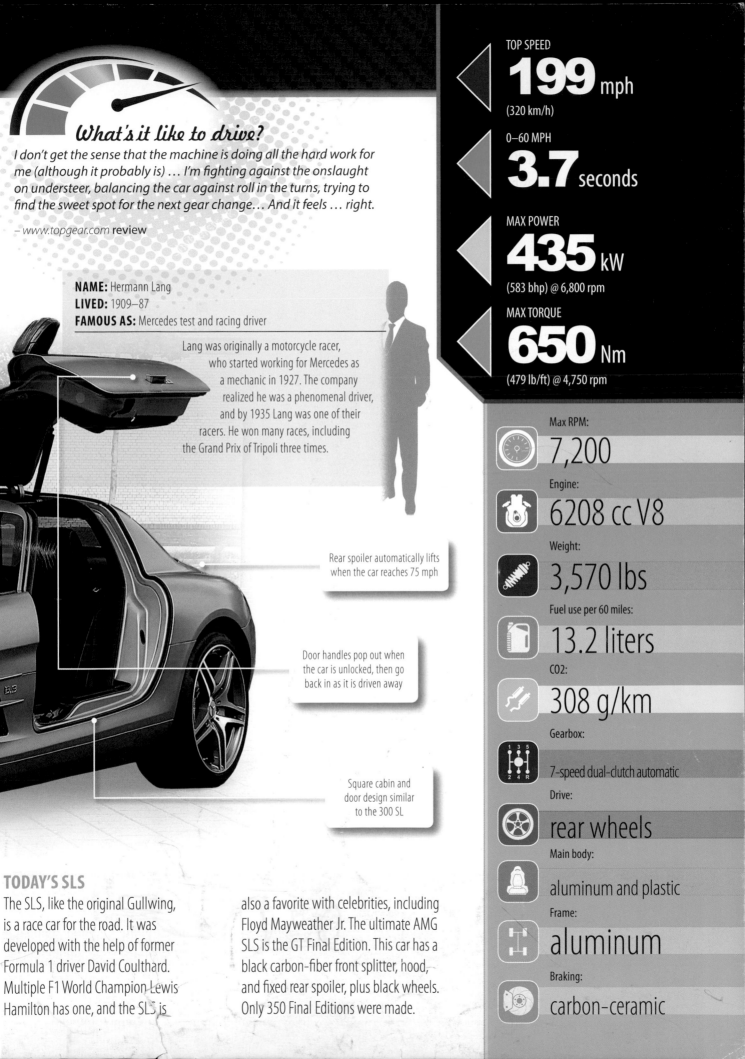

What's it like to drive?

I don't get the sense that the machine is doing all the hard work for me (although it probably is) … I'm fighting against the onslaught on understeer, balancing the car against roll in the turns, trying to find the sweet spot for the next gear change… And it feels … right.

– www.topgear.com **review**

NAME: Hermann Lang
LIVED: 1909–87
FAMOUS AS: Mercedes test and racing driver

Lang was originally a motorcycle racer, who started working for Mercedes as a mechanic in 1927. The company realized he was a phenomenal driver, and by 1935 Lang was one of their racers. He won many races, including the Grand Prix of Tripoli three times.

Rear spoiler automatically lifts when the car reaches 75 mph

Door handles pop out when the car is unlocked, then go back in as it is driven away

Square cabin and door design similar to the 300 SL

TODAY'S SLS

The SLS, like the original Gullwing, is a race car for the road. It was developed with the help of former Formula 1 driver David Coulthard. Multiple F1 World Champion Lewis Hamilton has one, and the SLS is also a favorite with celebrities, including Floyd Mayweather Jr. The ultimate AMG SLS is the GT Final Edition. This car has a black carbon-fiber front splitter, hood, and fixed rear spoiler, plus black wheels. Only 350 Final Editions were made.

TOP SPEED
199 mph
(320 km/h)

0–60 MPH
3.7 seconds

MAX POWER
435 kW
(583 bhp) @ 6,800 rpm

MAX TORQUE
650 Nm
(479 lb/ft) @ 4,750 rpm

Max RPM:
7,200

Engine:
6208 cc V8

Weight:
3,570 lbs

Fuel use per 60 miles:
13.2 liters

CO2:
308 g/km

Gearbox:
7-speed dual-clutch automatic

Drive:
rear wheels

Main body:
aluminum and plastic

Frame:
aluminum

Braking:
carbon-ceramic

PORSCHE
911 GT3 RS

The 911 is probably the most famous, most dreamed-about car Porsche makes. If you ever had a poster of a Porsche on your wall, it was probably a 911. The GT3 RS is the ultimate 911.

The 911 first appeared in 1963, and ever since it has been popular with drivers who want to go extremely fast. In fact, in 2007 a 911 driver became Britain's fastest speeder when he was caught by police doing 172 mph. He was sent to prison for 10 weeks.

The 911 was originally designed as a 2+2 road car. The GT3 RS is great on the road, and good – if not better – on the racetrack. This version is lighter, more powerful, faster, and has better aerodynamics than any 911 before. It is, as one reviewer said, "one of the finest Porsches ever."

DOWNFORCE AT SPEED

The faster you go in a GT3 RS, the more downforce the car creates. At 186 mph, the front splitter and wheel-arch vents create 242 lbs of downforce on the front wheels. At the back, the huge rear wing and other aerodynamic features add 485 lbs of downforce. This is a total of 727 lbs — the same as having four adult men sitting on the roof. (If they could hang on at 186 mph.)

Vents release air behind front wheel arches, lowering air pressure inside the arches and doubling downforce

What's it like to drive?

Mostly we were concentrating on having fun without ending our day in a wall. This we accomplished thanks to the RS's rock-steady stability, neutral handling, and otherworldly grip.

– First-drive review on www.caranddriver.com

Splitter draws air in below nose of car

GT3 RS TIMELINE

1959	1963	1998	2015
Ferdinand Porsche draws the first designs for the 911	The first 911s go on sale in Germany: has a flat-6, air-cooled engine which, like the VW Beetle, is mounted at the back	The first liquid-cooled 911s go on sale – Porsche fans everywhere shed a tear because the traditional air-cooled engine sound has gone forever	The Porsche GT3 RS is released

In theory, a 911 GT3 RS will cost you a minimum of $190,000 — but there is a long waiting list. In 2015, a UK dealer advertised a used car that had been driven 141 miles for $429,000. The price was so high, he said, because, "this is a car you can actually drive away today."

Larger, 21-inch rear wheels mean the GT3 RS's nose is tilted slightly downward

Gearbox changes gear automatically in 95 milliseconds (0.095 second)

The GT3 RS has rear-wheel steering (the front wheels also steer, of course). It is the first Porsche to have this system.

seco

MAX POWER

368 kW

(493 bhp) @ 8,250 rpm

MAX TORQUE

460 Nm

(339 lb/ft) @ 6,250 rpm

Max RPM:
8,800

Engine:
3996 cc flat-6

Weight:
3,300 lbs

Fuel use per 60 miles:
12.7 liters

CO2:
296 g/km

Gearbox:
7-speed dual-clutch automatic

Drive:
rear wheels

Main body:
carbon fiber and **magnesium** alloy

Frame:
aluminum

Braking:
carbon-ceramic

NAME: Ferdinand Porsche
LIVED: 1875–1951
FAMOUS AS: Car designer

Ferdinand Porsche worked for Daimler and Mercedes-Benz, and in 1934 he designed the Volkswagen Beetle. After World War II, Volkswagen agreed to make him a small payment for every Beetle they sold. As over 20 million of Porsche's Beetles were eventually sold, this worked out well. In 1959, Porsche's grandson, whose name was also Ferdinand, drew the first designs for a car that would be even more famous than the Beetle: the 911.

PORSCHE
9FF GT9

Porsches are generally known to be pretty fast already — but they can be faster! In Dortmund, a company called 9ff turns standard Porsches into street-legal race cars. The GT9 is their fastest car.

The GT9 is based on a Porsche 911. 9ff makes several different versions of the GT9, depending on what the buyer wants the car to do.* The fastest version, the Vmax, was one of the first road cars ever to go more than 250 mph. It was recorded traveling at 272 mph. Another version, the Amax, is designed for maximum acceleration. It reaches 186 mph in fewer than 13 seconds — about as long as a Ford Fiesta takes to reach 60 mph.

A RARE SUPERCAR
Only 20 of the original GT9 Vmax cars were ever made, and no two GT9s are exactly the same. Each buyer chooses their own trim for the inside, and could have a stereo, air conditioning, and other optional extras added.

Factory: Dortmund, North Rhine-Westphalia, Germany

Price Tag...

You can't buy one, at least not new: they were all sold very quickly. The price of a new GT9 Vmax was more than $1 million. For a car faster than a Bugatti Veyron, this may seem reasonable. On the other hand, for a car without air conditioning, or even a stereo, it may seem like quite a lot.

Twin-turbo engine mounted in the middle of the car

Carbon-fiber body panels, doors, etc. reduce weight by almost 660 lbs

Engine air intake is gold plated, to make sure air going in is as cool as possible

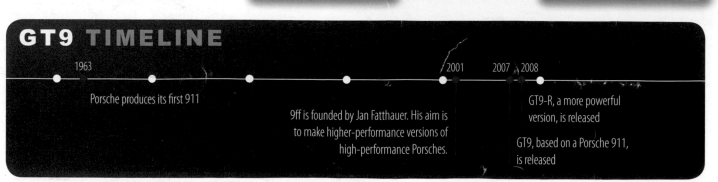

GT9 TIMELINE

1963 — Porsche produces its first 911

2001 — 9ff is founded by Jan Fatthauer. His aim is to make higher-performance versions of high-performance Porsches.

2007 — GT9, based on a Porsche 911, is released

2008 — GT9-R, a more powerful version, is released

*The data here is for the standard version.

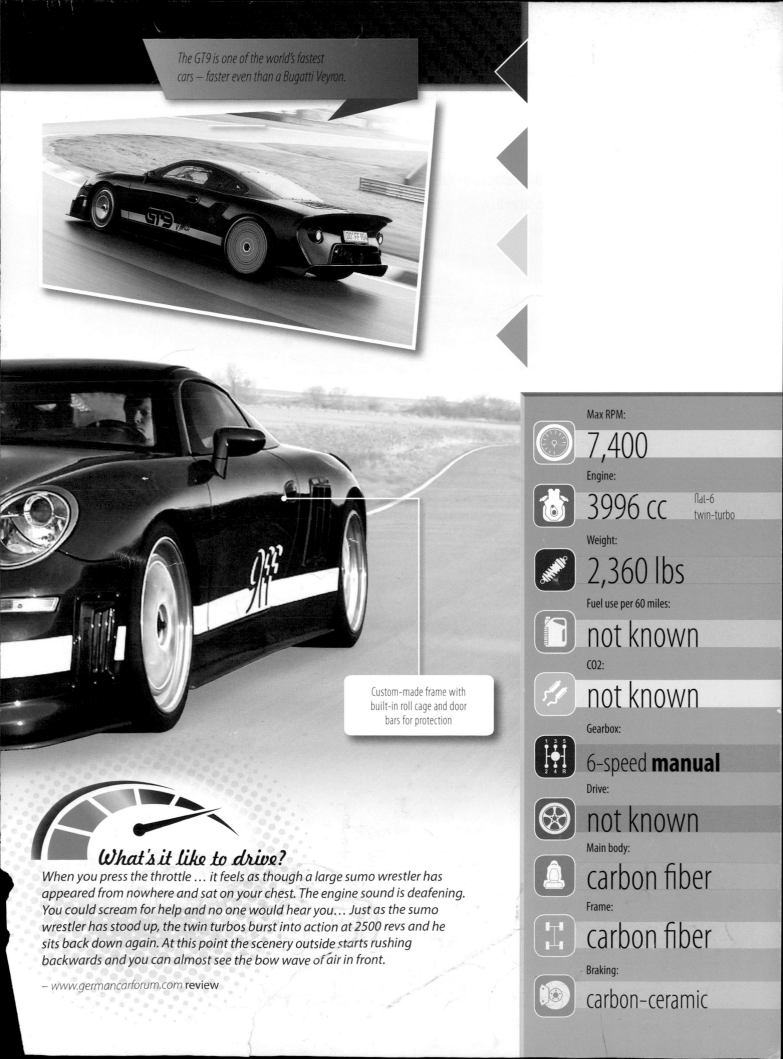

The GT9 is one of the world's fastest cars — faster even than a Bugatti Veyron.

Custom-made frame with built-in roll cage and door bars for protection

What's it like to drive?

When you press the throttle … it feels as though a large sumo wrestler has appeared from nowhere and sat on your chest. The engine sound is deafening. You could scream for help and no one would hear you… Just as the sumo wrestler has stood up, the twin turbos burst into action at 2500 revs and he sits back down again. At this point the scenery outside starts rushing backwards and you can almost see the bow wave of air in front.

– www.germancarforum.com **review**

Max RPM:
7,400

Engine:
3996 cc   flat-6 twin-turbo

Weight:
2,360 lbs

Fuel use per 60 miles:
not known

CO2:
not known

Gearbox:
6-speed **manual**

Drive:
not known

Main body:
carbon fiber

Frame:
carbon fiber

Braking:
carbon-ceramic

PORSCHE
918 SPYDER WEISSACH

In 2013, a Porsche 918 Spyder set off around the famous Nürburgring racetrack. After 6 minutes and 57 seconds, it crossed the finish line. It had smashed the record for the fastest lap by a road car.

Factory: Stuttgart, Baden-Württemberg, Germany

The car that broke the Nürburgring record was not just any Porsche Spyder — it was a Weissach edition. Compared to the original car, the Weissach is lighter and faster, with improved aerodynamics. The Weissach looks super-cool too, with a paint job that is a reminder of the racing Porsches of the 1970s.

Roof, rear spoiler, mirrors and windshield frame are all carbon fiber, reducing weight

GAS-ELECTRIC POWER

Like every 918 Spyder, the Weissach is a hybrid-power car; running off gas and electricity. For gas power it has a snorting **normally aspirated** V8 engine. It gets an extra boost of power from two electric motors, one for each axle. The electric battery can be fully charged in fewer than 30 minutes.

The Spyder's exhaust pipes point up from the engine. One test driver described them as sounding "like the arrival of a swarm of very angry mutant horror wasps, played through AC-DC's sound system."

Price Tag...

It will cost you in the region of $1 million, and that's before you start adding extras such as a stereo or air conditioning.

918 SPYDER WEISSACH TIMELINE

2004
Porsche releases the Carrera GT, like the 918 a mid-engined supercar. It is powered by a V10 gas engine.

2013
The first 918 Spyder gas-electric hybrid goes on sale

2015
After 918 cars have been sold, production of the 918 Spyder ends

What's it like to drive?

I turned the knob to Sport Hybrid mode and heard the sonic boom. And then I went for the full-fat Race Hybrid setting and it felt as though I were slingshotting round the moon.

– Jeremy Clarkson on *www.driving.co.uk*.

Carbon blades improve aerodynamics

Magnesium wheels reduce weight by 33 lbs

TOP SPEED
214 mph
(345 km/h)

0–60 MPH
2.6 seconds

MAX POWER
652 kW
(874 bhp) @ 8,500 rpm

MAX TORQUE
1280 Nm
(944 lb/ft) @ 6,700 rpm

Max RPM:
9,150

Engine:
4593 cc — V8 plus two electric motors

Weight:
3,600 lbs

Fuel use per 60 miles:
3.0 liters

CO2:
70 g/km

Gearbox:
7-speed dual-clutch automatic

Drive:
all 4 wheels

Main body:
carbon fiber

Frame:
carbon fiber

Braking:
carbon-ceramic

NAME: Walter Röhrl
LIVED: 1947–present
FAMOUS AS: Race and rally driver; Porsche test driver

One of the world's best ever rally drivers, Röhrl was once described by Niki Lauda as a "genius on wheels". Coming from a three-time Formula 1 World Champion, this comment really means something. After retiring from racing, Röhrl became a test driver for Porsche. He is now their chief test driver, and has helped develop many of Porsche's most famous supercars.

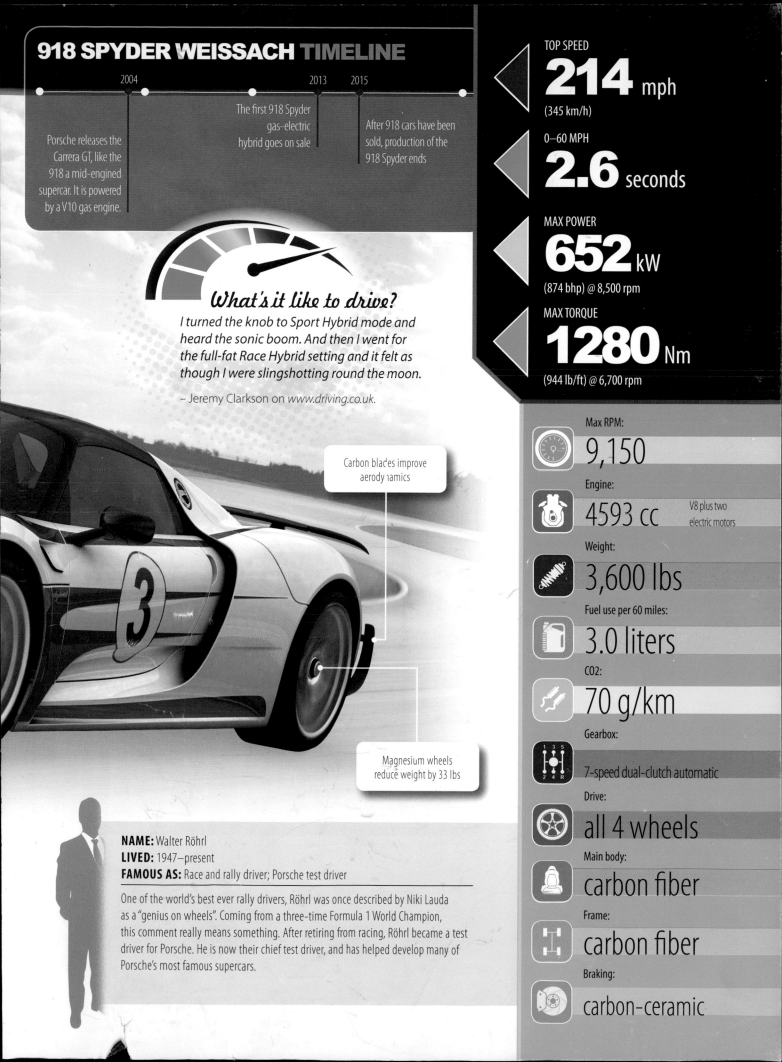

PORSCHE
718 BOXSTER S

Factory: Stuttgart, Baden-Württemberg, Germany

Most Porsche supercars have the engine at the back. The Boxster is different: it is **rear-mid engined**. Many drivers feel that this makes the Boxster one of the best-handling Porsches you can get.

Having the engine further forward shares its weight more equally between all four wheels. More weight on the wheels gives the tires more grip. This makes the Boxster a lot of fun to drive fast on a winding road.

The 718 Boxster S features a turbo-charged **flat-4** engine – different from the flat-6 which powers most Porsches. To begin with fans were outraged, but fortunately the Boxster S turned out to be completely wonderful to drive.

*The Porsche 718 S has an **ergonomic**, sporty interior, with a choice of finishes.*

S·GO 2700

What's it like to drive?

You put your foot down and feel your internal organs [being] squeezed to one side under the sheer g-force … it can throw you at the horizon with sufficient force to make you feel physically uncomfortable.

– review by autocar.co.uk

BOXSTER S TIMELINE

1957	1969	2010	2016

The 914 is released: a mid-engined, targa-topped sports car

The Boxster Spyder is released

The 718 Spyder race car appears. Many of its design features are also seen on the modern 718 Spyder.

Boxster S, with a new flat-4 turbo-charged engine instead of a traditional Porsche flat-6

Note: data is for an automatic car with Sport Chrono extras.

Optional "launch" control button: drivers push this when they want to do the fastest possible start

"Comfort" and "sport" mode selector: sport is aimed at racetracks and smooth, fast roads

Roll bars behind seats are made of mixed steel and aluminum

Roll bar for windshield is made of steel

TOP SPEED

17.7 m (/h)

PH

.2 se

ER

57 k

(345 bhp) @ 6,500 rpm

MAX TORQUE

420 N

(310 lb/ft) @ 1,900 rpm

Max RPM:
7,400

Engine:
2497 cc   flat-4 turbo

Weight:
3,055 lbs

Fuel use per 60 miles:
7.3 liters

CO2:
167 g/km

Gearbox:
6-speed manual or 7-speed dual-clutch automatic

Drive:
rear wheels

Main body:
steel/aluminum

Frame:
steel/aluminum

Braking:
aluminum (carbon-ceramic optional)

DOWN ON POWER, UP ON THRILLS

The Boxster S has less than half the power of a 918 Spyder Weissach. However, it has a stripped-out cabin (Porsche even replaced the door handles with fabric loops to reduce weight), lightweight **bucket seats**, and some of the soundproofing material removed. With the optional manual gearbox, it feels like a totally modern version of an old-fashioned street-racing car.

Price Tag...

In the world of supercars, the 718 S is a bit of a bargain: it starts at about $75,000. This means for the same cost as a single 918 Weissach, you could buy eleven 718 Spyders and still have enough money left over for a dream vacation.

OTHER GERMAN SUPERCARS

The supercars in this book are some of the newest, fastest, and most exciting supercars made in Germany. But lots of other amazing German supercars have recently been manufactured. Here are a few of them:

MANUFACTURER: LOTEC
MODEL: C1000
YEAR: 1995

As rare as a supercar can be: only one was ever made. It was built for a wealthy oilman from the United Arab Emirates, and was said to have cost him $3.4 million. Rumors say it reached 268 mph, making it one of the world's fastest cars.

MANUFACTURER: MERCEDES
MODEL: CLK-GTR
YEAR: 1997

Like the Porsche 911 GT1 Strassenversion, the CLK-GTR was built as a **homologation** special. Only 25 were made: Mercedes kept the first one, so only 24 were ever sold. The race car was designed for GT1 and Le Mans 24-Hour racing, and the road version was almost identical.

MANUFACTURER: MERCEDES
MODEL: SL65 AMG BLACK SERIES
YEAR: 2008

As Mercedes said, "Limited production. Unlimited performance." The raw statistics of 60 mph in 3.8 seconds and a limited top speed of 199 mph show that the SL65 was a real supercar.

MANUFACTURER: PORSCHE
MODEL: CARRERA GT
YEAR: 2004

The Carrera GT is sometimes described as one of the last supercars without lots of electronic driver aids. With a targa top and a 612 bhp, V10-engine, only 1,270 of these were ever made.

MANUFACTURER: PORSCHE
MODEL: 911 GT1 STRASSENVERSION
YEAR: 1996

Porsche built just 25 road-going versions of this car, making it super rare. Built to satisfy homologation rules for GT-class racing, this really is a race car you can drive on the road.

MANUFACTURER: PORSCHE
MODEL: 996 GT1
YEAR: 1996

This road-going version of Porsche's race car had a classic flat-6 engine and would hit 60 mph in 3.6 seconds. You could buy one for around $528,000, as long as you didn't expect things like interior trim or a stereo.

MANUFACTURER: MERCEDES
MODEL: SLR MCLAREN
YEAR: 2003

Before McLaren became a supercar manufacturer on its own, it worked with Mercedes. The ultimate result was the SLR. Several different versions were made, but the most wonderful to look at was the SLR Stirling Moss. This is a Batman-style version of an old open-cockpit racing car, the 1955 300 SLR (see page 30).

High-performance German cars were among the first to compete in races, in the early 1900s. Ever since, companies such as Mercedes, Porsche, and BMW have been building amazing cars for people who like to drive fast and look good. Here are just a few of the most famous German supercars from the past:

MANUFACTURER: BMW
MODEL: 507
YEAR: 1956

The 507 was a bit of a disaster for BMW. It cost too much to make, which meant it ended up costing buyers twice as much as planned. Despite being popular with celebrities (Elvis Presley had one), only 252 were ever made. Today, only 202 are known to survive: each is worth over $1 million.

MANUFACTURER: MERCEDES BENZ
MODEL: SL300 GULLWING
YEAR: 1954

So beautiful it makes you want to cry, the Gullwing was also an extremely high-performance car. It was the world's fastest road car and a multiple race winner.

MANUFACTURER: MERCEDES BENZ
MODEL: 300 SLR
YEAR: 1955

The great British driver Stirling Moss drove a 300 SLR in the 1955 World Sportscar Championship. The championship was six races long, and Moss missed the first two. He then won three of the last four races: the **Mille Miglia**, RAC Tourist Trophy and the **Targa Florio**. Mercedes won the manufacturers' prize.

MANUFACTURER: PORSCHE
MODEL: 356
YEAR: 1948

The 356 is powered by an 1100 cc flat-4 engine, and hardly counts as a supercar. But this was the first Porsche ever and even today you can tell it's a Porsche.

MANUFACTURER: PORSCHE
MODEL: 914
YEAR: 1970

The 914 was a joint development between Porsche and Volkswagen, known as the "VW Porsche." The 914 was mid-engined (unlike most rear-engined Porsches), but was available with a classic flat-6 Porsche engine. To save weight, some parts of the bodywork were fiberglass.

GLOSSARY

2+2 car with two main seats in the front and two small, usually uncomfortable seats behind

aerodynamics how air flows around an object

axle rod connecting the wheels on opposite sides of a car

bucket seat seat with a rounded back that fits around your sides, which holds you in place when going around a corner at high speed

composite made up of several materials

concept car a car built to test or show a new design

convertible car design where the roof can fold down

coupe car with a fixed, solid roof, two doors and a sloping rear

downforce downward pressure on the tires, which makes them grip the road better

drive system providing power to the wheels, for example rear-wheel drive, front-wheel drive, and all-wheel drive

ergonomic designed to maximize comfort and performance

flat-4/6 engine with four or six cylinders arranged in two horizontal rows (lying flat), with two or three cylinders in each row

Formula E series of races for electric-powered cars

homologation rules that allow a car to be entered in a particular race category. Usually a certain number of that particular car must be sold for use on the road.

hybrid a type of engine that uses power from more than one source, usually in cars an internal combustion engine combined with electric motors.

inline 5 engine with five cylinders arranged all in a row

LED short for Light-Emitting Diode, a kind of bright-white light used in some car headlights

magnesium alloy metal that is lighter, stronger and better at absorbing vibration than aluminum

manual gears the driver has to change for himself or herself, using a gearstick

mid-mounted describes an engine that is behind the driver and passenger seats, where its weight helps all four wheels grip the road

Mille Miglia translated as "thousand miles," the Mille Miglia is a famous Italian race held on public roads between 1927 and 1957

monocoque a special vehicle frame that gets its strength from its outer layer, instead of a supporting frame (*monocoque* = "single cell" in French)

normally aspirated engine that is not fitted with turbo chargers

Nürburgring world-class motorsports track and facilities in Nürburg, Germany

rear-mid engine with the engine behind the driver but in front of the rear wheels

safety car car driven around in front of a line of racing cars to slow them down, if there has been an accident during a race

stop-start system computer-controlled system for stopping a car when it is not moving, then restarting it again when the driver wants to move off. Stop-start systems are a way of saving fuel and causing less pollution.

street legal allowed to be driven on public roads

Targa Florio motor race held in the mountains of Sicily between 1907 and 1977

torque the amount of "work" exerted by an engine

track day when ordinary drivers can pay to drive on a racetrack. Sometimes a race car and instruction from a racing driver are part of the experience.

WRC short for World Rally Championship

FURTHER INFORMATION

Books

Crum, Colin. *Porsche vs. Lotus*. New York, NY: Windmill Books, 2014.

Goldsworthy, Steve. *Scorching Supercars*. North Mankato, MN: Capstone Press, 2015.

Phillips, Adam. *Supercars*. New York, NY: Rosen Publishing, 2013.

Website

PowerKids Press has developed an online list of websites related to the subject of this book. This site is updated regularly. Please use this link to access the list: www.powerkidslinks.com/sc/german

I. PLAINTIFF'S MOTION FOR SUMMARY JUDGMENT IS PROPERLY BEFORE THE COURT.

In an unlawful detainer action a motion for summary judgment may be made on five days' notice. C.C.P. Sec. 1170.7. The time limits imposed by subdivision (a) of section 437c, as well as the requirement in subdivision (b) of a separate statement of material facts not in dispute, are not applicable to summary judgment motions in unlawful detainer actions. C.C.P. Sec. 437c(r).

The "separate statement" requirement for summary judgment motions does not apply to unlawful detainer actions. C.C.P. Section 437c, subdivision (r), states: "Subdivisions (a) and (b) do not apply to actions brought pursuant to Chapter 4 (commencing with section 1159) of Title 3 of Part 3." The latter refers to the unlawful detainer statutes, and the requirement for a separate statement of facts is in section 437c(b). Thus, C.C.P. Section 437c(r) expressly states, though by an obscure reference to its own subdivision (b) and to C.C.P. Sections 1159 et seq., that unlawful detainer summary judgment motions do not require a separate statement of facts contended to be undisputed. While Rule 3.1350, California Rules of Court, is silent on this issue, to construe such silence as requiring a separate statement of undisputed facts in unlawful detainer summary judgment motions, notwithstanding C.C.P. Section 437c(r), would allow a rule of court to supersede a statute, which is not permitted.

In all other respects, the motion is required to be granted on the same terms and conditions as a summary judgment motion under C.C.P. Sec. 437c, and such a motion must be decided solely on the affidavits or declarations filed. Ibid, subd. (c).

II. PLAINTIFF HAS ESTABLISHED THE PRIMA FACIE ELEMENTS OF AN UNLAWFUL DETAINER ACTION FOR NONPAYMENT OF RENT.

Under section 1162(a)(2) of the Code of Civil Procedure, a tenant or subtenant is guilty of unlawful detainer

> When he continues in possession ... after default in the payment of rent ... and three days' notice, in writing requiring its payment, stating the amount which is due, or possession of the property, shall have been served on him ....

Elements other than default in rent, service of the notice, the expiration of three days without payment, and the continuance in possession include the existence of a landlord-tenant relationship (Fredricksen v. McCosker (1956) 143 Cal. App. 2d 114) and proper contents of the notice (Wilson v. Sadleir (1915) 26 Cal. App. 357, 359). Plaintiff's declaration establishes all these elements, so that plaintiff is entitled to summary judgment.

III. DEFENDANT(S) CANNOT PREVAIL UNDER A DEFENSE OF BREACH OF THE IMPLIED WARRANTY OF HABITABILITY.

Under the rule of <u>Green v. Superior Court</u> (1974) 10 Cal. 3d 616, the California Supreme Court held that in an unlawful detainer action founded on nonpayment of rent, the tenant could assert as a defense that the landlord breached an implied warranty to keep the premises habitable. The Court cited with approval the case of <u>Hinson v. Delis</u> (1972) 26 Cal. App. 3d 62 in this regard. In <u>Hinson</u>, the tenant sued the landlord in a regular civil action for breach of this implied warranty. After the trial court ruled in favor of the landlord, the Court of Appeal reversed, holding that there existed such a warranty in the law, as to which, "The tenant must also give notice of alleged defects to the landlord and allow a reasonable time for repairs to be made." <u>Hinson</u> at p. 70. When the <u>Green</u> court held that the warranty of habitability established by the <u>Hinson</u> court could be asserted by the tenant as a defense to an unlawful detainer action, as well as a basis for suit by the tenant, it did not modify or remove this requirement of notice by the tenant to the landlord of the alleged defects by which the tenant seeks to withhold rent. Therefore, the notice requirement also applies where the defense is asserted by the tenant in an unlawful detainer action.

Plaintiff's declaration establishes that defendant(s) failed to give plaintiff notice of the alleged defects in the premises. Unless a triable issue of fact exists in this regard, defendant(s) cannot assert this defense, as a matter of law.

Date: _____ , _____

_____
Plaintiff in Pro Per

PROOF OF PERSONAL SERVICE
(C.C.P. § 1011 (b))

1

2

3   I the undersigned, declare:

4   I am over the age of 18 years and not a party to the within action.

5   On _____ , _____ , I served the within Notice of Motion for Summary

6   Judgment, Declaration of Plaintiff, and Points and Authorities on defendant(s) by delivering true copies thereof to each

7   such defendant, or other person not less than 18 years of age, at defendants' residence address of _____

8   _____ , City of

9   _____ , California, between 8:00 A.M. and 6:00 P.M.

10   I declare under penalty of perjury under the laws of the State of California that the foregoing is true and correct.

11

12   Date:_____ , _____   _____
                                                Signature

13

14

15

16

17

18

19

20

21

22

23

24

25

26

27

28

1   Name:

        Address:

2

        Phone:

3

        Plaintiff in Pro Per

4

5

6

7

8   SUPERIOR COURT OF CALIFORNIA, COUNTY OF _____

9   _____ DIVISION

10

11   _____)   Case No. _____

             Plaintiff,   )

12   )   ORDER GRANTING MOTION

     v.   )   FOR SUMMARY JUDGMENT

13   )

  _____)

14   Defendant(s).   )

  _____)

15

16   Plaintiff's motion for summary judgment came on for hearing in Department _____ of

17   the above-entitled Court on _____ , _____ , said plaintiff appearing in pro per and

18   defendant(s) _____ appearing by _____ . The

19   matter having been argued and submitted,

20   IT IS HEREBY ORDERED that plaintiff's motion for summary judgment for restitution of the premises the subject of this

21   action, rent and damages in the sum of $ _____ , and costs of suit be, and the same is, granted.

22

23   Date: _____ , _____

24   _____

                                         Judge of the Superior Court

25

26

27

28

1   Name:
     Address:

2

     Phone:

3

     Plaintiff in Pro Per

4

5

6

7

8   SUPERIOR COURT OF CALIFORNIA, COUNTY OF _____

9   _____ DIVISION

10

11 _____)   Case No. _____

           Plaintiff,   )

12   )   JUDGMENT FOLLOWING GRANTING
     v.   )   OF MOTION FOR SUMMARY JUDGMENT

13   )
_____)

14   Defendant(s).   )
_____)

15

16   The motion of plaintiff for summary judgment having been granted,

17   IT IS HEREBY ORDERED AND ADJUDGED that plaintiff have and recover from defendant(s) _____

18   _____

19   possession and restitution of the real property located at _____

20   _____ , City of _____ ,

21   County of _____ , California, rent and damages in the sum of

22   $ _____ , plus costs of suit in the sum of $ _____ , for the total sum of $ _____ .

23

24   Date:_____ , _____

25   _____
                          Judge of the Superior Court

26

27

28

PLAINTIFF:	CASE NUMBER:
DEFENDANT:	

JUDGMENT—UNLAWFUL DETAINER ATTACHMENT

7. ☐ **Conditional judgment.** Plaintiff breached the covenant to provide habitable premises to defendant.

    a. ☐ Defendant must pay plaintiff a reduced rent because of the breach in the amount and for the period shown below. *(Specify each defect on a separate line, the month or months (or other period) that the defect existed, and the percentage or amount of the reduced rent as a result of the defect to arrive at the reasonable value of the premises for the period that the defect or defects existed.)*

Month defect existed	Defect	Reasonable rental value is reduced by *(specify percentage)* or *(specify amount)*		Reduced monthly rent due
(1)		%	$	$
(2)		%	$	$
(3) ☐ Continued on *Attachment* 7a (form MC-025).		%	$	$
	Total rent due in the 3-day notice is now *(specify):*			$

    b. ☐ Defendant is entitled to attorney fees *(specify):* $ and costs *(specify):* $.

    c. ☐ Defendant is the prevailing party if defendant pays plaintiff *(specify total rent in item 7a, less any attorney fees and costs in item 7b):* $ by   p.m. on *(date):*   at *(address):*

    d. ☐ Judgment will be entered for defendant when defendant has complied with item 7c shown ☐ by defendant's filing of a declaration under penalty of perjury (see form MC-030), with proof of service on the plaintiff, OR ☐ at a hearing that has been set in this court as follows:

Date:	Time:	Dept.:	Room:

        (1) ☐ Defendant must continue to pay rent after expiration of the 3-day notice if the defendant continues in possession of the premises in the amount of $ per month. The total rent at item 7a is the corrected amount under the 3-day notice.

        (2) ☐ Plaintiff must repair the defects described in item 7a. The court retains jurisdiction over the case until those repairs are made. Rent remains reduced in the amount of *(specify monthly rent)* $ until the repairs are made.

        (3) ☐ Rent will increase to *(specify monthly rent)* $ the day after

           ☐ plaintiff files a declaration under penalty of perjury (see form MC-030), with proof of service on the defendant, stating that all the repairs have been made OR ☐ it is established that all the repairs have been made at a hearing set in this court as follows:

Date:	Time:	Dept.:	Room:

    e. ☐ Plaintiff is the prevailing party if defendant fails to comply with items 7c and 7d.

Form Approved for Optional Use
Judicial Council of California
UD-110S [New January 1, 2003]

JUDGMENT—UNLAWFUL DETAINER ATTACHMENT

Code of Civil Procedure, § 1174.2
Civil Code, §§ 1941, 1942.3

f. ☐ Judgment will be entered for plaintiff ☐ when plaintiff files a declaration under penalty of perjury (see form MC-030), with proof of service on the defendant, that the amount in item 7c has not been paid, OR ☐ at a hearing that has been set in the court as follows:

Date:	Time:	Dept.:	Room:

(1) ☐	Past-due rent *(item 7a)*		$
(2) ☐	Holdover damages *		$
(3) ☐	Attorney fees *(item 7b)*		$
(4) ☐	Costs *(item 7b)*		$
(5) ☐	Other *(specify):*		$
(6)	**TOTAL JUDGMENT**		$

*Use one of the following formulas: From expiration of the 3-day notice to ☐ today's date ☐ date the premises were vacated *(specify number of days)* times

☐ *(specify reduced monthly rent $*   times 0.03228 *(12 months divided by 365 days).)*

☐ *(specify reduced rent per month divided by 30): $*

= Total holdover damages

g. ☐ Plaintiff is awarded possession of the premises located at *(street address, apartment, city, and county):*

h. ☐ The rental agreement is canceled.   ☐ The lease is forfeited.

8. ☐ **Other** *(specify):*

ATTORNEY OR PARTY WITHOUT ATTORNEY *(Name, state bar number, and address):*

FOR COURT USE ONLY

TELEPHONE NO.:   FAX NO.:

ATTORNEY FOR *(Name):*   Plaintiff in Pro Per

NAME OF COURT:

STREET ADDRESS:

MAILING ADDRESS:

CITY AND ZIP CODE:

BRANCH NAME:

PLAINTIFF:

DEFENDANT:

APPLICATION AND ORDER FOR APPEARANCE AND EXAMINATION

CASE NUMBER:

☐ **ENFORCEMENT OF JUDGMENT**   ☐ **ATTACHMENT (Third Person)**
☐ **Judgment Debtor**   ☐ **Third Person**

ORDER TO APPEAR FOR EXAMINATION

1. TO *(name):*
2. YOU ARE ORDERED TO APPEAR personally before this court, or before a referee appointed by the court, to
   a. ☐ furnish information to aid in enforcement of a money judgment against you.
   b. ☐ answer concerning property of the judgment debtor in your possession or control or concerning a debt you owe the judgment debtor.
   c. ☐ answer concerning property of the defendant in your possession or control or concerning a debt you owe the defendant that is subject to attachment.

Date: Time: Dept. or Div.:   Rm.:

Address of court ☐ shown above ☐ is:

3. This order may be served by a sheriff, marshal, registered process server, **or** the following specially appointed person *(name):*

Date:

_____
JUDGE OR REFEREE

This order must be served not less than 10 days before the date set for the examination.

IMPORTANT NOTICES ON REVERSE

APPLICATION FOR ORDER TO APPEAR FOR EXAMINATION

4. ☐ Judgment creditor   ☐ Assignee of record   ☐ Plaintiff who has a right to attach order
   applies for an order requiring *(name):*   to appear and furnish information
   to aid in enforcement of the money judgment or to answer concerning property or debt.
5. The person to be examined is
   a. ☐ the judgment debtor.
   b. ☐ a third person (1) who has possession or control of property belonging to the judgment debtor or the defendant or (2) who owes the judgment debtor or the defendant more than $250. An affidavit supporting this application under Code of Civil Procedure section 491.110 or 708.120 is attached.
6. The person to be examined resides or has a place of business in this county or within 150 miles of the place of examination.
7. ☐ This court is **not** the court in which the money judgment is entered or *(attachment only)* the court that issued the writ of attachment. An affidavit supporting an application under Code of Civil Procedure section 491.150 or 708.160 is attached.
8. ☐ The judgment debtor has been examined within the past 120 days. An affidavit showing good cause for another examination is attached.

I declare under penalty of perjury under the laws of the State of California that the foregoing is true and correct.

Date:

▶

_____
(TYPE OR PRINT NAME)

_____
(SIGNATURE OF DECLARANT)

(Continued on reverse)

**APPLICATION AND ORDER
FOR APPEARANCE AND EXAMINATION**
(Attachment—Enforcement of Judgment)

Code of Civil Procedure,
§§ 491.110, 708.110, 708.120

APPEARANCE OF JUDGMENT DEBTOR (ENFORCEMENT OF JUDGMENT)

NOTICE TO JUDGMENT DEBTOR If you fail to appear at the time and place specified in this order, you may be subject to arrest and punishment for contempt of court, and the court may make an order requiring you to pay the reasonable attorney fees incurred by the judgment creditor in this proceeding.

APPEARANCE OF A THIRD PERSON
(ENFORCEMENT OF JUDGMENT)

(1) NOTICE TO PERSON SERVED If you fail to appear at the time and place specified in this order, you may be subject to arrest and punishment for contempt of court, and the court may make an order requiring you to pay the reasonable attorney fees incurred by the judgment creditor in this proceeding.

(2) NOTICE TO JUDGMENT DEBTOR The person in whose favor the judgment was entered in this action claims that the person to be examined pursuant to this order has possession or control of property which is yours or owes you a debt. This property or debt is as follows *(Describe the property or debt using typewritten capital letters)*:

If you claim that all or any portion of this property or debt is exempt from enforcement of the money judgment, you must file your exemption claim in writing with the court and have a copy personally served on the judgment creditor not later than three days before the date set for the examination. You must appear at the time and place set for the examination to establish your claim of exemption or your exemption may be waived.

APPEARANCE OF A THIRD PERSON (ATTACHMENT)

NOTICE TO PERSON SERVED If you fail to appear at the time and place specified in this order, you may be subject to arrest and punishment for contempt of court, and the court may make an order requiring you to pay the reasonable attorney fees incurred by the plaintiff in this proceeding.

APPEARANCE OF A CORPORATION, PARTNERSHIP, ASSOCIATION, TRUST, OR OTHER ORGANIZATION

It is your duty to designate one or more of the following to appear and be examined: officers, directors, managing agents, or other persons who are familiar with your property and debts.

Questionnaire For Judgment-Debtor Examination

Date of Examination: _____, 20 _____

Part 1. Basic Identifying Facts

Your full name: _____

Any other names (including married/maiden names) used by you: _____

_____

Are you married?: _____ If so, give your spouse's full name: _____

If married, what other name(s) has your spouse used? _____

Your current residence (not P.O. box) address: _____

_____

Your telephone numbers: Home: _____ Work _____

Do you have any children? _____ If so, give their names and ages, and state whether they live with you:

_____

_____

_____

Part 2a. Employment of Debtor

Are you employed? _____ Your employer's name and address: _____

_____

_____

How long have you worked for this employer? _____

What is your job classification? _____

Rate of pay? $_____ gross per month $_____ per hour. Hours per week you work for this employer: _____

What are your job duties? _____

Do you receive any kind of incentive payments or bonuses from your employer? _____

If so, state the conditions under which you get them, and when you get them:

_____

_____

_____

Part 2b. Employment of Spouse

Is your spouse employed? _____ Employer's name and address: _____

_____

_____

_____

How long has she/he worked for this employer? _____

©nolo   NOLO

What is his/her job classification? _____

Rate of pay? $_____ gross per month $_____ per hour. Hours per week she/he works for this employer: _____

What are his/her job duties? _____

Does she/he receive any kind of incentive payments or bonuses from the employer? _____

If so, state the conditions under which she/he gets them, and when she/he gets them: _____

_____

_____

_____

Part 2c. Other Employment of Debtor or Spouse

Your employer's name and address: _____

_____

_____

How long have you worked for this employer? _____

What is your job classification? _____

Rate of pay? $_____ gross per month $_____ per hour. Hours per week you work for this employer: _____

What are your job duties? _____

Do you receive any kind of incentive payments or bonuses from your employer? _____

If so, state the conditions under which you get them, and when you get them: _____

_____

_____

_____

Part 2d. Self-Employment of Debtor or Spouse

If you or your spouse is engaged in any type of full- or part-time self-employment, give the name and type of business, and its location:

_____

_____

_____

How long in this business? _____ Did you or your spouse start up or purchase it? _____

If started up, when? _____

If purchased, state the purchase price, date of purchase, and full names and addresses of sellers: _____

_____

_____

_____

Do you or your spouse have an accountant for this business? _____

Accountant's name and address: _____

_____

_____

Who prepares your business and personal income tax returns? _____

_____

Part 3. Cash, Savings or Checking Accounts, Safe Deposit Boxes

How much cash do you have on your person right now? _____

Do you or your spouse have a checking account? _____

If so, give bank, S&L, or credit union name and branch: _____

_____

Do you have a checkbook with you now? _____ If yes, give the account number(s): _____

Who is authorized to sign checks on the account? _____

_____

What is the current approximate balance? $_____ When did you make your last deposit? _____

Amount of last deposit: $_____ How often do you make deposits? _____

How often does your spouse make deposits? _____

When did you write your last check on that account? _____ How much was the check for? $_____

Do you or your spouse have a savings account? _____

If so, give bank, S&L, or credit union name and branch: _____

_____

State the account number(s): _____

Who is authorized to withdraw funds? _____

_____

What is the current approximate balance? $_____ When did you make your last deposit? _____

Amount of last deposit? $_____ When did you last make a withdrawal? _____

Do you have access to any business account for which you are an authorized signer? _____

Give the bank or S&L name, branch, and business name and address: _____

_____

Do you or your spouse have a safe deposit box? _____

Who has access to the box? _____

What property is kept in it? _____

_____

_____

Give the box location and number: _____

_____

Part 4. Motor Vehicles

What motor vehicles do you and your spouse drive?

Vehicle 1: Make: _____ Model: _____ Year: _____

License Plate Number: _____ State: _____

Registered Owner(s): _____

_____

Where garaged? _____

Est. Value: $_____ Is it fully paid for? _____ If not paid for, state amount owed: $ _____

Name and address of lender/lienholder/legal owner: _____

_____

_____

Vehicle 2: Make: _____ Model: _____ Year: _____

License Plate Number: _____ State: _____

Registered Owner(s): _____

_____

Where garaged? _____

Est. Value: $_____ Is it fully paid for? _____ If not paid for, state amount owed: $ _____

Name and address of lender/lienholder/legal owner: _____

_____

_____

Do you or your spouse own any recreational vehicles, such as campers, trailers, boats, dirt bikes, and so on ? _____

If yes, give the following information:

Type of Vehicle: _____ Model: _____ Year: _____

License/Registration Number: _____ State: _____

Registered Owner(s): _____

_____

Where kept? _____

Est. Value: $_____ Is it fully paid for? _____ If not paid for, state amount owed: $ _____

Name and address of lender/lienholder/legal owner: _____

_____

_____

Part 5. Current Residence

Do you live in an apartment, single-family house, mobile home, condominium unit, or townhouse? _____

Do you rent or own your home? _____

Part 5a. If Debtor Rents

How much rent do you pay? $ _____ When paid? _____

How do you pay; check, cash, or money order? _____

Do you rent out any rooms? If so, state rents received and names of persons paying: _____

_____

_____

_____

State landlord's name, address, and phone: _____

_____

_____

_____

How long have you rented at this address? _____

Part 5b. If Debtor and/or Spouse Own Home

Who is listed as owner(s) on the deed to the property? _____

_____

When was the home purchased? _____ What was the purchase price? $_____

How much was the down payment? $_____ How much are the monthly payments? $_____

To what bank, S&L, or mortgage company are the monthly payments made_____

_____

Who makes the actual payments? _____

How are the payments made: cash, check, or money order? _____

How much is still owed on the loan? $_____

How much do you think the property could sell for today? $_____

Is there a second deed of trust or second mortgage against the property? _____

For what amount? $_____ How much are the monthly payments? $_____

Who are these payments paid to? _____

Are there any other liens against the property? _____

If so, state the amounts, the names of the lienholders, and how the liens occurred: _____

_____

_____

Do you rent out any of the rooms in the residence? _____ If so, state rents received and names of persons paying:

_____

_____

_____

Part 6. Real Property Other Than Home

Do you or your spouse own any real estate anywhere (other than any already discussed in 5b above)? _____

If yes, what kind of property is it? (vacant land? commercial property? and so on): _____

_____

_____

Is there a structure of any type on the land? _____ If yes, what kind? _____

Who is listed as owner(s) on the deed to the property? _____

When was the property purchased? _____

_____

What was the purchase price? $_____ How much was the down payment? $_____

How much are the monthly payments? $_____

To what bank, S&L, or mortgage company are the monthly payments made? _____

_____

_____

Who makes the actual payments? _____

How are the payments made: cash, check, or money order? _____

How much is still owed on the loan? $_____

How much do you think the property could sell for today? $_____

Is there a second deed of trust or second mortgage against the property? _____ For what amount? $_____

How much are the monthly payments? $_____

Who are these payments paid to? _____

Are there any other liens against the property? _____

If yes, state the amounts, the names of lienholders, and how the liens occurred _____

_____

_____

_____

Do you receive any rents from the property? _____ If so, state rents received and names of persons paying:

_____

_____

_____

_____

Part 7. Other Property

Do you or your spouse own any stocks, bonds, or corporate securities of any kind? _____

If yes, state corporation name and address, type of holding, name(s) of owner(s), and value of holding(s):

_____

_____

_____

Do you or your spouse own any deeds of trust or mortgages on any real property or personal property? _____

If yes, state nature of property, location, nature of payments to you, and location of property:

_____

_____

_____

Are there any unsatisfied judgments in favor of you or your spouse? _____

If yes, state plaintiffs and defendants, amount of judgment, court, county, and judicial district: _____

_____

_____

_____

Do you or your spouse own any rings, watches, diamonds, other jewelry or antiques of any kind worth $100 or more? _____

If yes, list property and value: _____

_____

_____

_____

Do you or your spouse own any other personal property not already discussed, that is worth over $100? _____

If yes, list property and value: _____

_____

_____

_____

In the past year have you or your spouse received any payments of money other than already discussed? _____

If yes, state amounts, dates received, reason money was received, and what happened to the money: _____

_____

_____

_____

Are you the beneficiary in any will? _____

If yes, state name and address of author of will, relationship of that individual to you, and type and value of property to be received:

_____

_____

Part 8. Business Relations and Employment History

Are you or your spouse an officer, director, or stockholder of any corporation? _____

If yes, state corporation's name and address, nature of business, your or your spouse's position, and the nature and value of any shares of stock owned: _____

_____

_____

_____

For the past five years, list names and addresses of all businesses conducted by you and employment had by you, giving your position, duration of employment, and rate or amount of pay:

_____

_____

_____

_____

_____

_____

_____

_____

_____

_____

_____

_____

_____

_____

_____

_____

_____

_____

ATTORNEY OR PARTY WITHOUT ATTORNEY (Name, State Bar number, and address):	LEVYING OFFICER (Name and Address):

TELEPHONE NO.:   FAX NO.:
E-MAIL ADDRESS:
ATTORNEY FOR (Name):

SUPERIOR COURT OF CALIFORNIA, COUNTY OF
STREET ADDRESS:
MAILING ADDRESS:
CITY AND ZIP CODE:
BRANCH NAME:

PLAINTIFF/PETITIONER:

DEFENDANT/RESPONDENT:

COURT CASE NUMBER:

APPLICATION FOR EARNINGS WITHHOLDING ORDER
(Wage Garnishment)

LEVYING OFFICER FILE NUMBER:

TO THE SHERIFF OR ANY MARSHAL OR CONSTABLE OF THE COUNTY OF:
OR ANY REGISTERED PROCESS SERVER

1. The judgment creditor (name): requests
issuance of an Earnings Withholding Order directing the employer to withhold the earnings of the judgment debtor (employee).
    Name and address of employer   Name and address of employee

2. The amounts withheld are to be paid to   Social Security no. ☐ on form WG-035 ☐ unknown
  a. ☐ The attorney (or party without an attorney)   b. ☐ Other (name, address, and telephone):
     named at the top of this page.

3. a. Judgment was entered on (date):_____
   b. Collect the amount directed by the Writ of Execution unless a lesser amount is specified here: $ _____

4. Check any that apply:
  a. ☐ The Writ of Execution was issued to collect delinquent amounts payable for the **support** of a child, former spouse, or spouse of the employee.
  b. ☐ The Writ of Execution was issued to collect a judgment based entirely on a claim for elder or dependent adult financial abuse.
  c. ☐ The Writ of Execution was issued to collect a judgment based in part on a claim for elder or dependent adult financial abuse. The amount that arises from the claim for elder or dependent adult financial abuse is (state amount): $ _____

5. ☐ Special instructions (specify):

6. Check a or b:
  a. ☐ I have not previously obtained an order directing this employer to withhold the earnings of this employee.
     —OR—
  b. ☐ I have previously obtained such an order, but that order (check one):
     ☐ was terminated by a court order, but I am entitled to apply for another Earnings Withholding Order under the provisions of Code of Civil Procedure section 706.105(h).
     ☐ was ineffective.

▶

_____ (TYPE OR PRINT NAME)   _____ (SIGNATURE OF ATTORNEY OR PARTY WITHOUT ATTORNEY)

I declare under penalty of perjury under the laws of the State of California that the foregoing is true and correct.
Date:

▶

_____ (TYPE OR PRINT NAME)   _____ (SIGNATURE OF DECLARANT)   **Page 1 of 1**

Form Adopted for Mandatory Use
Judicial Council of California
WG-001 [Rev. January 1, 2012]
APPLICATION FOR EARNINGS WITHHOLDING ORDER
(Wage Garnishment)
Code Civ. Procedure, § 706.121
www.courts.ca.gov

ATTORNEY OR PARTY WITHOUT ATTORNEY (Name, State Bar number, and address):

After recording return to:

TELEPHONE NO.:

FAX NO. (Optional):

E-MAIL ADDRESS (Optional):

ATTORNEY FOR (Name):   Plaintiff in Pro Per

SUPERIOR COURT OF CALIFORNIA, COUNTY OF

STREET ADDRESS:

MAILING ADDRESS:

CITY AND ZIP CODE:

BRANCH NAME:

FOR RECORDER'S OR SECRETARY OF STATE'S USE ONLY

PLAINTIFF:

DEFENDANT:

CASE NUMBER:

ACKNOWLEDGMENT OF SATISFACTION OF JUDGMENT

☐ **FULL**   ☐ **PARTIAL**   ☐ **MATURED INSTALLMENT**

FOR COURT USE ONLY

1. Satisfaction of the judgment is acknowledged as follows:
   a. ☐ Full satisfaction
      (1) ☐ Judgment is satisfied in full.
      (2) ☐ The judgment creditor has accepted payment or performance other than that specified in the judgment in full satisfaction of the judgment.
   b. ☐ Partial satisfaction
      The amount received in partial satisfaction of the judgment is $
   c. ☐ Matured installment
      All matured installments under the installment judgment have been satisfied as of (date):

2. Full name and address of judgment creditor:*

3. Full name and address of assignee of record, if any:

4. Full name and address of judgment debtor being fully or partially released:*

5. a. Judgment entered on (date):
   b. ☐ Renewal entered on (date):

6. ☐ An ☐ abstract of judgment ☐ certified copy of the judgment has been recorded as follows (complete all information for each county where recorded):

COUNTY	DATE OF RECORDING	INSTRUMENT NUMBER

7. ☐ A notice of judgment lien has been filed in the office of the Secretary of State as file number (specify):

NOTICE TO JUDGMENT DEBTOR: If this is an acknowledgment of full satisfaction of judgment, it will have to be recorded in each county shown in item 6 above, if any, in order to release the judgment lien, and will have to be filed in the office of the Secretary of State to terminate any judgment lien on personal property.

▶

Date:

(SIGNATURE OF JUDGMENT CREDITOR OR ASSIGNEE OF CREDITOR OR ATTORNEY**)

Page 1 of 1

*The names of the judgment creditor and judgment debtor must be stated as shown in any Abstract of Judgment which was recorded and is being released by this satisfaction. ** A separate notary acknowledgment must be attached for each signature.

Form Approved for Optional Use
Judicial Council of California
EJ-100 [Rev. January 1, 2005]

ACKNOWLEDGMENT OF SATISFACTION OF JUDGMENT

Code of Civil Procedure, §§ 724.060, 724.120, 724.250

POS-020

ATTORNEY OR PARTY WITHOUT ATTORNEY *(Name, State Bar number, and address):*

TELEPHONE NO.:   FAX NO. *(Optional):*

E-MAIL ADDRESS *(Optional):*

ATTORNEY FOR *(Name):*

SUPERIOR COURT OF CALIFORNIA, COUNTY OF

STREET ADDRESS:

MAILING ADDRESS:

CITY AND ZIP CODE:

BRANCH NAME:

PETITIONER/PLAINTIFF:

RESPONDENT/DEFENDANT:

CASE NUMBER:

PROOF OF PERSONAL SERVICE—CIVIL

(Do not use this Proof of Service to show service of a Summons and Complaint.)

1. I am over 18 years of age and **not a party to this action**.
2. I served the following **documents** *(specify):*

☐ The documents are listed in the *Attachment to Proof of Personal Service—Civil (Documents Served)* (form POS-020(D)).

3. I personally served the following **persons** at the address, date, and time stated:
   a. Name:
   b. Address:
   c. Date:
   d. Time:

☐ The persons are listed in the *Attachment to Proof of Personal Service—Civil (Persons Served)* (form POS-020(P)).

4. I am
   a. ☐ not a registered California process server.
   b. ☐ a registered California process server.
   c. ☐ an employee or independent contractor of a registered California process server.
   d. ☐ exempt from registration under Business & Professions Code section 22350(b).

5. My name, address, telephone number, and, if applicable, county of registration and number are *(specify):*

6. ☐ I declare under penalty of perjury under the laws of the State of California that the foregoing is true and correct.
7. ☐ I am a California sheriff or marshal and certify that the foregoing is true and correct.

Date:

▶

_____   _____
(TYPE OR PRINT NAME OF PERSON WHO SERVED THE PAPERS)   (SIGNATURE OF PERSON WHO SERVED THE PAPERS)

Form Approved for Optional Use
Judicial Council of California
POS-020 [New January 1, 2005]

PROOF OF PERSONAL SERVICE—CIVIL

Code of Civil Procedure, § 1011
www.courtinfo.ca.gov

INFORMATION SHEET FOR PROOF OF PERSONAL SERVICE—CIVIL

(This information sheet is not a part of the Proof of Service form and does not need to be copied, served, or filed.)

NOTE: This form should **not** be used for proof of service of a summons and complaint. For that purpose, use *Proof of Service of Summons* (form POS-010).

Use these instructions to complete the *Proof of Personal Service* (form POS-020).

A person at least 18 years of age or older must serve the documents. There are two main ways to serve documents: (1) by personal delivery and (2) by mail. Certain documents must be personally served. You must determine whether personal service is required for a document.

The person who personally served the documents must complete a proof of service form for the documents served. **You cannot serve documents if you are a party to the action.**

INSTRUCTIONS FOR THE PERSON WHO SERVED THE DOCUMENTS

The proof of service should be printed or typed. If you have Internet access, fillable versions of the form are available at *www.courtinfo.ca.gov/forms*.

Complete the top section of the proof of service form as follows:

<u>First box, left side</u>: In this box print the name, address, and phone number of the person *for* whom you served the documents.

<u>Second box, left side</u>: Print the name of the county in which the legal action is filed and the court's address in this box. The address for the court should be the same as on the documents that you served.

<u>Third box, left side</u>: Print the names of the Petitioner/Plaintiff and Respondent/Defendant in this box. Use the same names as are listed on the documents that you served.

<u>First box, top of form, right side</u>: Leave this box blank for the court's use.

<u>Second box, right side</u>: Print the case number in this box. The number should be the same as the case number on the documents that you served.

Complete all applicable items on the form:

1. You are stating that you are over the age of 18 and that you are not a party to this action.

2. List the name of each document that you delivered to the person. If you need more space, check the box in item 2, complete the *Attachment to Proof of Personal Service—Civil (Documents Served)* (form POS-020(D)), and attach it to form POS-020.

3. Provide the name of each person served, the address where you served the documents, and the date and time of service. If you served more than one person, check the box in item 3, complete the *Attachment to Proof of Personal Service—Civil (Persons Served)* (form POS-020(P)), and attach it to form POS-020.

4. Check the box that applies to you. If you are a private person serving the documents for a party, check box "a."

5. Print your name, address, and telephone number. If applicable, include the county in which you are registered as a process server and your registration number.

6. You must check this box if you are not a California sheriff or marshal. You are stating under penalty of perjury that the information you have provided is true and correct.

7. Do not check this box unless you are a California sheriff or marshal.

At the bottom, fill in the date on which you signed the form, print your name, and sign the form at the arrow. By signing, you are stating under penalty of perjury that all the information that you have provided on form POS-020 is true and correct.

Proof of Service by Mail

My address is _____

_____ , California.

On _____ , 20_____ , I served the within: _____

_____

_____

_____

by depositing true copies thereof, enclosed in separate, sealed envelopes, with the postage thereon fully prepaid, in the

United States Postal Service mail in _____ County, addressed as follows:

_____

_____

_____

_____

_____

_____

_____

_____

_____

_____

_____

_____

I am, and was at the time herein-mentioned mailing took place, a resident of or employed in the County where the

mailing occurred, over the age of eighteen years old, and not a party to the within cause.

I declare under penalty of perjury under the laws of California and of the United States of America that the foregoing is

true and correct.

Date: _____ , _____

_____

Signature

Index

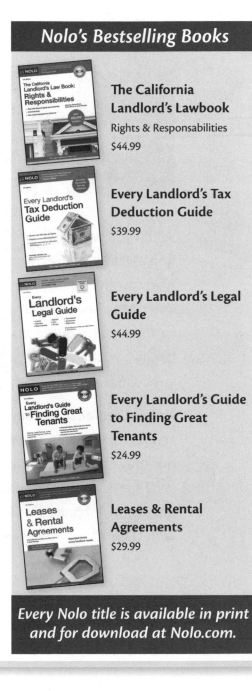